A Beggar's Loom

Matt Santateresa

A Beggar's Loom

The Mansfield Press

Canadian Cataloguing in Publication Data

Santateresa, Matt, 1950-
A Beggar's Loom

Poems
ISBN 1-894469-07-0

1. Title
PS8587.A3739B43 2001 C811'.54 C2001-902264-6
PR9199.3.S224B43 2001

Acknowledgements:

The author gratefully acknowledges the following magazines and journals in which poems in *A Beggar's Loom* first appeared: Amethyst Review, Prism, Quarry, Queen Street Quarterly, Qwerty, Symposium and Zygote.

Cover and text design by Darren Holmes
Cover photo by Paul Beard

Printed in Canada

Mansfield Press Inc. has been generously supported by the Canada Council and the Government of Canada through the Book Publishing Industry Development Program.

The Canada Council for the Arts
Le Conseil des Arts du Canada

Mansfield Press Inc.
25 Mansfield Avenue, Toronto, Ontario, Canada, M6J 2A9
Publisher: Denis De Klerck

For my parents, Matteo and Muriel

Contents

General Wolfe at Quebec, c. 1760 3

Letter from Baudelaire to Jeanne Duvall, Honfleur, 1859 4

Shoemaker-Levy 9, July 18, 1994 5

Aubade Nude, Upper Lachine Rd., August 1999 6

Night Locusts, Hockey Riot, Montreal 7

A First-Time Home Owner Considers Ridding the Basement of Spiders 8

Great Paris Exhibition 1900 9

From the Law Office of Williamson & Walton, Mussey Building, Washington, D.C., 1940 10

A Seventeen Year Old Gazes Out A Tenement on Mulberry Street, NYC, 1943 11

Ectopic 12

Baudelaire on Mme Sabatier, 1843 13

A Minister's Calling: Automatic Car Wash 14

1969, LSD-25, McGill Ghetto, 2:30 AM 15

First and Last Song to the English Lake District, 1859 16

Phillippe Hebert, Quebecois Sculptor in NYC, c.1870 17

Giles Corey, Danvers, Mass., c.1690 18

The Blue Note, NYC, c.1950 20

The Chambermaids of St. Lawrence Hall, Mid-morning, c.1864 21

Baudelaire 22

Lascaux 23

J.W. Booth's Last Letter from Zekiah Marsh, c.1865 24

1963 & Zapruder 25

Negative Capabilities: A Voyeur Romance, 1819 26

Auction, Hemmingford, Quebec 28

Glen Miller, July 13, 1997 29

Lines Composed on Pine Hill 30

Wittgenstein 32

Notes Toward A Pastoral 33

The Notion of War in St. Alban's, Vermont, Being an Eye Witness Account Following the Confederate Raid of October, 1864 34

History Beach Motel, Gloucester, Mass. 36

Road to Plaster Rock 37

Upon Reading Montale's 'Lemon Trees' 39

Witnessing What Appears at Paradise Lake 40

Chagall 41

Ending the Contract that Begins with I, 1964 42

Franconia 43

Riding the Rivets in Eden 44

You must tell people how to live 45

Water 46

Ballet Dancers' Feet 47

Nanotechnology, after Bill Joy 48

Mr. Martin, Pianist from Estonia, In town for a Competition, Goes for a Smoke in the Ericssons' Backyard in Calgary, Canada, November, 2000 49

December 20th 2000 And A River 50

The Appearance of Things 51

A Beggar's Loom

General Wolfe at Quebec, c. 1760

behind the lines at midnight
scaling limestone cliffs

my blind hands grasp branches
chokecherry, breathing
like stone. *The bladder scalds, Katherine*
I just beheaded one of my men
who began to cry, ropes of blood
over rock

ravens whisper your name
wings encircle my head

Letter from Baudelaire to Jeanne Duvall, Honfleur, 1859

Jeanne,
I am sick of alcohol, drugs
grown-up foods. It is blue-veined
breast milk I crave and need.
This weed I smoke
I will tear out by the roots.
These teeth
I will ply out to become biteless
so I will attach myself to you
curled, suckling

I'll return to elemental
primary verbs
a savaged mouth to suck,
suck eyes closed once again
eyes closed so tight
they will trust again, and sleep

sleep to flower in an open eye of heaven

Shoemaker-Levy 9, July 18, 1994.

Coming from nowhere
string of pearls that in a huff
a lover grasps and rips them off
her moonlit neck
they fling into a far orbit
angry with momentum
begin to spin in line toward
Jovian duff.

She powders her face in a hand-
held mirror, covers the bruise
a dust rises off her cheek
Q-comet hits the surface and
a plume delivers solace to aeons
of astronomers, its even-tempered
scales unfazed
but our world discovers its origin
in radio waves, colours, though
I can't tell from here if life were possible.

Commonplace, along this night road
listening to informative voices
like a first language explain the universe.

All lights are punched out.
The black sky fills with insomniac stars.
This road is abandoned, behind a grove
of black trees.

It makes little difference to calculations
from a grocery clerk or the windshield
of this car, a wet brown rogue leaf cloys
to its transience.

Turn the wipers on, a stubborn leaf
blocks out Jupiter.

Giotto's comet sits quietly beside me in moonlight.

Aubade Nude, Upper Lachine Rd., August 1999

It falls from nowhere into view
where my focus was about trees or sky
fitting random thought to thought
and casually she emerged from a taxi nude
to an attention that quickens with
her barest step, tetherless

without a scarf to cover a thought
leaving the impression of absence
she saunters down the street
reciting her own rights aloud

in a repeated rhythm a girl skipping
home. It is madness to explain
what is the matter with plain old nudity
leaving one alone with romantic
notions, after she has gone
and disappeared
into the trees and skies
of antiquity, or her apartment

terror and regal splendour
indiscreet
form and light alike, or hustled

in perpetuity across
blank industrial park mornings

Night Locusts, Hockey Riot, Montreal

A throwback
to droves, herds, mobs
ham-handed pulse

the French Suite plays
in my mind, like Gould
in a recording studio entranced
dancing

as bottles break panes
obscenities grind rhythms
adrenaline races
blood pressure, Goth
and Vandal

jagged fires gouge windows

rogues egged on
their lungs, raw leather

sirens fog the air
snake through backstreets

she brushes past

a look long enough
to note a blue vein
that runs silent
down
the neck
of her dress

A First-Time Home Owner Considers Ridding the Basement of Spiders

I bring to this house signatures of possession
        but, in basement window wells, over dark pipes, corners
distress me. Webs shimmer, their sudden ominous appearance

leaves me no option, I aim a nozzle and press
        an aerosol can that fizzes and begins
to cover their dark existence, febrile legs
        igneous torsos, now white indentures

I watch them retract to implosion, godless
        into hard light, defensive nothings
that captured a darker imagination
        off-guard
and quickly toilet paper entombs them
        and I flush them into oblivion, swirling
away.

Years ago in my aunt's garden, their dewed
        webs, small prisms covered corners in sunlight
my aunt's articulate and large hands working
        polychrome flowers as I, blowing
across memory watched the fibrils tremble
        and glimmer like a sharkskin

Lord, how these carapaces shine in my gloved hand!

Great Paris Exhibition
1900

Henry Adams gazes into the dynamo's eye,
its pure rendering blaze, electric
vision, eclectic signs ushering in
the outlet of repression all around
young ladies crinoline and chafing
jabber and brim
and this, this forty foot cataclysm
that he saw overtake
even Freud, the Virgin herself
making all history bunk
and forgetful in comparison
to this new America
awakening to alarm
radios, night clubs, factories
adjoining all night pharmacies
expanding neutrality
making love new again
and everlasting

From the Law Office of Williamson & Walton, Mussey Building, Washington, D.C., 1940

Having to do with your invention, Mr. Haslet
Excuse me, a fly is battering against the pane
Annoying, I realize it's poor letter etiquette
But your patent infringes on others, all the same

Hitler has taken Poland and the Czechs, Mr. Haslet
And you want to invent a new bobby pin, unless
You change the fulcrum or any portion you've got
Of the spring loop or pivot, you're dead, I guess

Like my brother in Idaho, preparing for this fucking war
Preparing to die I figure, already under siege. Excuse me
I got carried away, regrettably, entertain no bore
Of a patent unless major changes to history occur.

Reinvent man's nature, modify his instincts
Then you've got something original, worthwhile.

A Seventeen Year Old Gazes Out A Tenement on Mulberry Street, NYC, 1943

By now the boys have landed on a beach screaming
against death.

My mother is sending money to Italy.
Not for war, but love. Her lover is still a cobbler there.

She sends him money. Father found out. He will leave soon for
Montreal with another woman. Abandon us.

A son will be born to him. Mother is dreaming of him in Italy,
helicopters tiny as moths move across his flanks

Their slow pinwheel blades making the sound of grief
And gunfire as she puts the grenade pins in at the

Munitions factory each day and goes home after dark.

Inhale a Lucky Strike and watch kids masquerade
Across the street. Can't help but think of soldiers' blue

Lips in sand, face down, as tanks and companies roll on
Evolve deep inland toward capitals. They will never

Stop. I think of sex, thigh against thigh, the graves fill
One on top of the other. Fevered hands run across

Conquered women. Silver fighter planes roll gleaming
In the sun.

She smells sweet, her wet fluctuates, lubricates stars,
Galaxies. Smack another casing into morning, and bolt.

Ready to fire at will.

Ectopic

At the head of the stairs doubled over in pain.
    Paramedics transport her, a red strobe through the living
    room window.

Alfred took short desultory walks beside the Thames.
    Emily went into labour during Easter weekend and
*a sturdy looking boy was born Easter Sunday - dead; strangled at birth.**

Not even. Without a question without a word it would kill a
mother and given its leering shape would never live at any rate.

It is removed and bagged and burned up through the Auschwitz-
looking red brick hospital chimney.

Attracted by mid-19th century life as I am and
it has become immaterial, though some nights I dream of him
under transparent ice trying to break through and breathe, his
wide underwater eyes, his mouth pronouncing
his name, my name.

Dead as he was I felt proud of him.
*Today when I write this down, the remembrance of it rather overcomes me.**

*From the journals of Alfred Lord Tennyson

Baudelaire on Mme Sabatier, 1843

She sits naked at her Louis XIV dresser
and is seeing herself a few pounds lighter.
She makes sure her breasts are as full as before.

Sudden fur of a cat rubs her back
as she sits on the bed. Rolls back
and clasps the cat's sides, hoists
it above her head, snuggles into it
and goes under the sheets to doze.

A bigger body comes and spoons next to her.
A colder body, furless overpowers her
like a cabled animal. Muscular laugh
jacks her up with large hands above his groin
lowers her lightly, lifts her lightly. Both
are laughing and she shrieks as he squeezes
her sides, they wrestle to the floor, a jostle
of limbs knocking some furniture over like
pant-happy dogs scrambling in a room.
They forget their bruises, she carefully
stuffs a lightly perfumed handkerchief
in her mouth.

Hearing the fracas, B bangs on her door
asking if anything is the matter. Mme Sabatier
peaks over her sheets. Are you alright midons.
The cat scurries to a neutral corner from under
the covers. Curls into its haunch. Yes, I am alright.
There is nothing at all the matter.

B says she had a bad dream and advises her
not to sleep with that cat again.

A Minister's Calling: Automatic Car Wash

Call it 'tunnel vision', the way I entered the car wash
Following directions to the tee, 'Advance Slowly',
'Stop' or 'Back Up'. I notice the unevenly cut Playboy glossies
and magazine cut-outs; Neferititi, even a Dali.
I shudder as the cycle begins with a jetspray of water and soap to a
lather, the car moves through a blurred landscape the windshield
a thin scrimshaw of sorts, the chassis shakes
lightly, chamois tentacles begin to erase as large industrial
rollerbrushes wave across and to the sides in a
cradle of sound,
a baptismal dream and my mother
recently deceased is sitting in the passenger seat, limned
white, saying Mary sent her as her metaphor, to give
Faith. Faith is metaphor she says, not history, or fact, but
metaphor. And is this the desert?, I asked. Silence.
She places her cool hand on my forehead, calming me and she
becomes Raphael's Madonna but not my mother, blue and
white drapery, beatific smile
The car dries and moves through the tunnel toward the harsh
midday sunlight outside, hot air blowers like monotone biblical
trumpets evaporate the water beads on the hood, windshield, and
trunk
into a vision
you must live she says and disappears.

1969, LSD-25, McGill Ghetto, 2:30 AM

A violin concerto plays
on a Blaupunkt stylus
we sit on used bean bags
long-haired incense burns

strange russet notes emerge

matter is relaxed along an infinite curve

the Doors open on rows of gladiola-like forms
and transform to wasps that burst
into primordial reptiles and further

evolve, revolutionize
in a flash in a mirror

I am ape and master
and then sycophant mop
absorbing a world in voices
connected as a choir, forgiving
what it suffers brought to asylum

and my friends help raise me from the dead

First and Last Song to the English Lake District, 1859

Coleridge and Wordsworth walk
as menhirs philosophize
on edges of mouldering green.

Deep clouds reside over Ullswater
a patent sheen of a lake spreads, hones
imagination like a wind to rise

fathomless.

Throwing a hard flat stone
across it.

Phillippe Hebert, Quebecois Sculptor in NYC, c.1870

For years solitude reigns in the landscape
  the hills that roll in Laurentian bareness
like bodies only God forms, chiselled in shadows
  that stride out from the earth.
Shapes are the locus in stillness and in power.
  All curvature and edge. New York has nothing.
A language that scrapes the sky open and leaves
  me colder than a Megantic winter. These flower
seeds for sale door-to-door are miracles that stretch in
  elements temporarily housed for immaculate release
into space. Singular. Kicked open, alive.

Giles Corey, Danvers, Mass., c.1690

A courtroom swells with onlookers.
Tongues click in hysterical diction.
One of the accused lifts her skirt and
Slurps. Eyes turn away from her
Madness as she giggles uncontrollably.

First blamed were Sarah Good, Sarah
Osburn and Tituba. Execution followed
Execution between March 1 and September 22.
They said Tituba was a black witch with leather
Wings that spread to wrestle snakes or walk
Through fire.

I only saw my wife, judge, her eyes
Moist shimmer, her spinning in circles dervish-like
Chattering in strange tongues, her clothes
Passing through burning tapers placed methodically
On the floor. She began to foam at the mouth and
Collapsed unconscious in a heap.

Judge Hawthorne stares as a hubbub of accusation rises.

The next morning she convulsed as leaves coaxed
By a blue wind. Eyes rolling back, lips purple.

I see her, a pale young woman, walk
Along a path we knew years ago, leading
To a garden where we met.
And as I reach to touch her I pass through her
As if she were conjured
But I have no reason to rush away
Though scared witless, since nothing rises in me

As the time the children pointed out my guilt
As well, impossible to prove any innocence

At such time, minds a flame, but I forget
More and more, time blackens, senses fail
A whiff of urine in straw from my cell
A moment we coupled and no more.

Reverend Parris leads the way on horseback
Crowds jostle the ox-cart back and forth. I

Forget where exactly they dragged me, to
The outskirts, an open field.

Stone upon heavy stone pressing down
My chest finally broke, ears filled with
Blood. Then the sheriff takes his cane
And stuffs my tongue back into my mouth.
His eyes looking at whoever I was.

The Blue Note, NYC, c.1950

We finally tasted it, the way Kerouac et al
   would stay up drinking all night, talking
poetry and jazz, listening to Monk sweat
   bent over a piano, the notes joy makes as
he hums joining spheres from galaxies peripheral
   storms and counterpoints in earthy geometrics.

A sense of history takes precedent, looking
   around, a focus that penetrates cigarette smoke
surveying the premises, sipping a drink, we could see
      this strange man shaking his head with the music he plays
      Round about midnight

And then it was over, chairs turned up on tables, as always
   legs stuck up in air.

The Chambermaids of St. Lawrence Hall, Mid-morning, c.1864

are calling to each other across
the corridor of the oaken halls
and worn Persian carpets
in rich contraltos
as they luff fresh sheets
momentarily blocking sunlight
from the window

white shadows snap in laughter
that resonates in big rooms

generals from the South
were up to discuss strategies
cigar smoke densities
absorbed into linen

strategies for fatal pastures
in Virginia, flanking cliffs
in Pennsylvania, villages in
landscapes ringing out with
scalding bullets

scour a porcelain sink, she
spots a few drops of blood
from shaving

she fingers a mote and tastes it
and leaves
a bar of perfumed soap behind.

Baudelaire

Driving with black-leather-batting gloves on
through early morning sublimities
(it increases friction between a leather steering wheel
and my skin being smooth and dry, no fingerprints)

I remind myself of Baudelaire
making love with his kid gloves on
black-eyed Suzannes, voluptuous
senses heavens beyond facets
of sex, jeweled glistenings of
sweat across shoulders religion
small hills
fragile in solitude in deep morning air

o love along this empty road
open clear across the steamy green silent spiel

where a simple word can decompress
an entire expansive notion, decompose
into a violent act
that hits up along side
of the head
catching the ear
crowning its echo

with a ringing, tolling
in a distance
changeless and endless
and o what thirst it slakes in me

Lascaux

It is time.
The amygdala fires and neocortical associations
Smells as wet as minerals, and primordial I descend
into a cave

A pouch full of raw colours from plants
herbs, blood, and flints.

Crouch to avoid the stalactites, dodge
stalagmites, my feet bleed as I return
called before these unconscious walls
with

Ibex
Bear
Bison
Tiger

Still motion infuses them, I have
found the lines that makes them seem
to leap, run, across this stone sky

a taut haunch, an arm extends
to launch a spear, or talons clench

in flickering torchlight
I must move with this will that shapes
light itself
in my veins

that falls asleep
under their secure shapes,
immobile, moving

again and again.

J.W. Booth's Last Letter from Zekiah Marsh, c.1865

Because the trees are disconsolate and waver
    with moaning, like lyres Shakespeare wrote of
because it is April and spring begins
    to reach into deepest cells
of this leg that burns incessant, arms weakened, there
   are no flowers I can lug to your hearse or poem
I can write as Whitman, because no matter how long
    threnodies are, or sentences, they will not arrive
at any truth
    He knew one day an adversary would knock and
dispense him to a darkness, black as his stovepipe and suit, hair
        shoes, yes like lyres, those trees lament and frogs sing
over black miles
    as this pain gouges, and I draw from this silence
what I want to say and these words will have to do.

1963 & Zapruder

You could see clearly out the many
paned schoolroom window
how a fall blue vision was

no one ever died back then
grandparents were alive
and kept his photograph surrounded with
votive candles in their home shrines
his face ubiquitous on match covers

Mr. Mason our algebra teacher
his brain intact
his mortgage fully paid
stood before us spilling out
letters and numbers
an oratory aimed at finite solutions
and fixed values
his tweed sleeve chalky
with erasures in treating binomials
then Mrs. Walsh called him to the door
and he turned and announced that JFK had been shot

that cerulean day those exposed white
plosions flying bits
head jerking back, her panic-crawl
toward the black Lincoln trunk

Sandra sitting up front at her desk
went berserk, her tunic
flew up above her as she cried out
as if she were Magdelaine

a white brocaded waistband I recall
as white as that equal sign
that hung there on the board

Negative Capabilities: A Voyeur Romance, 1819

After a hard cough
and a hard look; a red thread-like
sanskrit letter curves across
a white pillowcase

hieroglyph of fate
from an eroded arterial wall
where angels tread
and impassively await getting worse
but for this roman window
harlequin doves toss themselves
into aerobic blue like syllables
of your name Fanny, that echo
and recall stalking voyeurs
bare footsteps up risers
like softest plummage
an object of primal urge

begins to disrobe, thin bodied
barely breathing from this distance

a place of artistic convenience
as if from behind a false mirror

take your time Fanny
absence makes it all the harder
to watch you untie your long auburn hair
angelic weight tossed to one side
over your shoulder

does art scavenge from these lit gaps?
bright windows in dark walls?
a reverence for light that loosens
nature's latent glory and by phases

lets fall, reveals beauty, truth?

Light drifts over your scapula
and a lovestruck boy is sent to heaven

until a stranger spots me lurking and
threatens me with constables who'll
come and arrest my indiscretions
ha! his property a barouche
for my imagination to apprehend
and restore a homeostatic inner voice

but the commotion has pulled the curtains
frisky as a forest creature leaping from icy
water, to dive under heavy medieval blankets
up to your eyes shiver

I am nothing but a hoodwinker hoodwinked
by his own stratagem, and you've become
anonymous, so I take this excitement
home, an image of adrenaline, alive

breathing hard.

Auction, Hemmingford, Quebec

If you didn't buy the oil lamp
or the eagle-headed butterdish
it didn't matter. What appeared
important was how the day was
passing.
Bankruptcy as socio-economic event.
Another's misfortune, our pleasure.
Refreshments served. Where is Rimbaud?
Da Vinci? With their 'I've solved this
problem, now what can I do? Where can I go?
The auctioneer pushes tarnished silverware.
Arthur had a mind to go, his poems
becoming limpid artifacts, no movement
other than a half rolled-up
roll-top desk in his African room.
I flip and flip through a 1900's photo album
of brown edged postcards from Europe, an
old medicinal smell, way back when
Gauguin was in Tahiti painting
all that he gave up for clerking.
I'm told a wife collected them, that she spent
her life in Hemmingford. On summer nights
she would return to the farm after a fair and
after having seen a dog with six legs chase a
stick. Her husband drunk, badgering her
for sex, opening her dress, she pushes him away
and leaves for home
once inside, she opens her album and returns
to Paris, Firenza, or London noise, symphony
traffic beyond what
she hears under him, meeting his demands.
She invents a theology far away
children shout, playing games
in Athens, Rome. She draws the muslin
curtains that luff in a street breeze
and the day passes like clouds
going for nothing, for a song.

Glen Miller, July 13, 1997
(Associated Press report by U. Ulfkotte)

Secrets keep appearance near perfect, now
as it was in the 40's, when Miller's band
left Paris, as atoms split into plosive orbits
Fermi's U-235 reaching critical mass and
contorted in ecstasy Miller died.
His listeners were many, my parents, yours
The awkward Kodak cameras that flashed
Believing his lovely wife tended home and garden
That fidelity was end-stopped and the family was first and
foremost...
We wonderfully forget that, Miller didn't and neither
are we about to lop off our trombones, become
monkish astronauts, no sir

'A Moonlight Serenade' played December 15, 1944
and he was presumed dead.
A thirty-three year jump cut
and a new story unwinds from the Associated Press:
Miller waits in a backseat, the sedan idles
a companion gives him the all-clear sign and he
gets out into a Paris drizzle, crosses a street and
enters a building rubs a woman's shoulder en passant,
exchanges smiles and continues up a spiral staircase, a
woman tenderly takes him by the elbow
and leads him in.

She scowls to remove him off her, mannequin
pushed aside, the companion, unnamed handles
the cover-up; celebrity, family man, hero, if we can say he
died in the crash with his band, *vous comprenez*
Memory still occupies a dance-floor, most of our parents
that knew him have died at any rate, died thinking
his songs were penultimate calls of theirs
skimming across hardwood floors in lovers arms, for moments
somehow immune and eternal.

Presently it is drizzling, the only difference is the weightlessness.
The key hangs in a front door. The small attachable
fan is silent and rests in potential.
Curtains are drawn and the news reports the trouble
with Mir in space, its biomedical/psychological problems.
A walk outside and
I notice that Something is always falling on leaves in a forest.
Out there, from deep skies the earth appears inconsequential, its
beauty
in shallow colours, our declared beauty, upon closer introspection,
is relative.
Flowers remain hidden and visible only as forest
green.
Invisible are these jonquils or irises that border the pond.

The beauteous forms that waylay senses
are large sweeps of one colour, and if not
in large quantities, as trees or water, are
forgettable, unsylvan, but for the broad
strokes of cerulean or emerald, nothing
in space but further fields for boredom's relief
under the notion of wonderful science.

I cannot hold this world too dearly as to want
never to leave, so I hear gunfire infuse a city
landscape, though note shooting stars as well
Hale-Bopp or Haley's, miracles that no longer
hold Giotto's forebodings, superstitions or an eclipse's
dragon, its stint as a moon-eater reduced to Something
falling in a forest..
On this hill; dogs bark and would indeed undo
my arm if let loose, or a sudden noise I make
in a wood
draw fire from a drunken hunter.

Even a beaver dam faces dynamite up here.
And streams that flow intermittent, have no
nymphs drink from them, nor are there remnants
of god. Except maybe a garbage pick-up on Thursdays

but I do remember a time, there was no question, no
opposition to the idea, at least
and now, for Christ's sake and the world's
this pastoral-like place is vacant, seen only
as an emerald green from the skies in love.

Wittgenstein
'All is flux'

Upon hearing of her hospitalization, I realize it
Makes little sense, the world at large, that is
The world is everything that is the case
Wittgenstein said - and decide to take him literally.
Tricks in perception; spores amalgamated there to burst
Despite Satan's Choice tomatoes poised
On a couple of 'hogs' that Walt Disney
Can turn into loveable facsimilies of
A Resurrection, or Giotto's nativity, even
Lear crosses at an intersection, broken and
Homeless, his highly valued opinions, calcified
Simply orders his cowering dog one way or
Another 'driveby' is taken away, critical condition
There may be glass that can flow through arteries
And lodge in her brain. Anesthetic calms her on
The table. Another cruel April, and humanity
Being treated like cartoon characters (can they
Run off cliffs, their feet running hopelessly in mid-
Air?)
Seven days later (for each dwarf) she manages
On Demerol, a bandaged head covers disfigurement
Her one good eye, a glaze, like a world's eye
Searches the space that surrounds it, frantic
To ascertain some familiarity
Like a whale's eye, an eerie look, of pathos and
Disturbance
And that is the case of everything in this world
she seems to say, spotting me

Notes Toward A Pastoral

A forest cottage, a diacrostic half-done in pencil
erasures, remnants, pages turned to unfinished
reading of novels

Clouds are passing, cast over
A mosquito huzzes indifferently near
forearm hairs, it is late August

there is nothing more to prey
a beaver slaps a dam, echoes carry
briefly

assume the young girl and boy are fucking
it is Eden

and I imagine the creature moves
toward the lilies, iris, as a dog barks
must be some human
tugs at his chain

straightens a tie on the way to work
leaves leaves and classical music behind

as well as birdsongs that flicker like psalms
hummingbirds, their tongues that indulge in properties

of yet another mottled language

and turns the ignition on.

The Notion of War in St. Alban's, Vermont, Being an Eye Witness Account Following the Confederate Raid of October, 1864

In their papers is about all, or maybe
a few teenagers went to fight for the Union
but like I said it was mostly the newspapers
their rows of names of the dead or their victories
and losses

There were vaults of maples that led up the hill
straight off the main street, you could gaze
up into them as you read

But that day, a couple of weeks ago, I remember
noticing smoke rising kind of steeply and quick
coming from the direction of The American House
our only hotel, I ran to see calling out for the brigade
as I ran, Ted, the butcher, Nat, the baker were surprised
as I was but they came to their senses as soon as
they saw the smoke and by then, flames were beginning
to gush from the windows and guests were coming out
the front door coughing and carrying on, come to think
of it, the smoke was blacker than usual, I remember
some Union soldiers a while back, showing us phosphorous
incendiary bombs, blackest smoke I ever
seen, it was pretty much the same

Practically the whole town was in front of the American
watching Franklin and the boys trying to squelch the fire
if that wasn't enough, of a sudden we hear howling and
yowling and turn to see a whole bunch of riders coming

down the street firing off their revolvers, as they approached we could
see they meant business, they
had masks on and got off their horses, in a dust about
as thick as the fire, and rushed into the bank a couple of doors
down from the American. I followed them in, one
was outside watching the horses, spotted me and told me to get
into the bank, talked with a southern drawl

Hands over my head, they were ransacking the safe
wordless and working at a fever's pitch, then one

said as he looked around eyeing everyone sort of military like and
waving a shotgun, he said don't anyone make a move we've come to
give you a taste of General Sherman's war then they all saddled up like
lightning and headed out of town

There was a crowd still gathered looking in amazement
at their dust leaving St. Alban's. Turning back to the fire
the smoke was blooming into all kinds of things; lions with black
flouting manes and what seem to be black
swans coupling

Got away to Montreal I hear
with about two hundred thousand.

History Beach Motel, Gloucester, Mass.

What is she doing in there all alone like some abandoned mother
cleaning?
I need that room that has all my wares to express love, dreams, the
closet wherein the breeze runs through herculean space where
there are 85, 000 feet holes
and the fishlines of imagination still run slack,
I've walked the beach 3 times and it's becoming old
Waves swing open and I memorize the antacid fizz
of seawater fading in sand, O I realize The Salvages
were written here and Olson fucked here along the docks
the whole historical distance performed as intimate
thoughts and deeds that fed needs over and over

She's taking her sweet time, hermetically sealing
our drinking glasses, our toilet seats

It's a painting, abstract, a Rothko

Sweeping away ashes, sand, scribblings that were hardly
endowed with the right memory, the right means become worthy of
disposal

Are waves applauding her leaving? I check quickly looking over my
shoulder

I see her impediment-cart outside my numbered room
she exits, all white, maternal, hallelujah

The room is restored to an original state, a language
empty of meaning except grace

that a window apprehends saying nothing
to disinherit the view
of waves and eeling shore
those constant reminders

Road to Plaster Rock

Our Corolla sends up a roostertail of dustmotes

in the passenger seat there is nothing
to do but stare at trees, titanium sunshine
corpuscular red flowers dot shoulders and ditches
kids in the backseat coordinate the medieval deaths
of computer images, the engine drones from its
metal cage and echoes across the woods

Michelangelo comes to mind, mindlessly,
especially his hospital apron, blood-stained
with his anatomical studies, his morbid
search for origins of muscular movement
then he is summoned by de Medici on a whim
to his villa in the countryside, Michelangelo
stares into sunlit Italian fields as an ox-cart travels
all he can see is a bearded face of an old peasant
who works with his scythe beside a rock
a rock that is roughly the peasant's size
the size of that man he dissected that morning

he unwraps his sculpting instruments and runs into
the field where he begins to chisel and later says
that the man was in the rock and he chiselled his
every muscle and sinew...

Further on, Van Gogh could have painted that Coke sign
riddled with rusting .22 bullet holes
it's all about God when you think about it, he'd say
charging the docile colours with a fusion
of carmine and milky loops of the logo
but trees would be virulent green rows of monastic swirls

shinto dervishes, their voices aflame licking titanium stars alive...

then at Saint-Paul-de-Mausole, the abbot visits the grounds not
realizing it is Van Gogh, stands over his stooped shoulder and watches
him painting; almost biblical the way he applies paint he thinks to
himself, like a limitless mind along the curves and then

the abbot remembers there are others to visit, sitting on cane
chairs rocking back and forth, crones, like sagging and decaying
pears,
both sexes
growing fuzz on their chins...

the kids in the backseat play as
Mozart's Sonata in 'F' is on the car radio
an arpeggio drives through the world outside
windows continuously open

Upon Reading Montale's 'Lemon Trees'

Perhaps poetry cannot take place
in Macdonald's where Oedipus sits
with his mother enjoying a refill

a chorus of children reminds
us that our dangers are almost always less
than we imagine

so panic comes under control
when fire breaks out in the kitchen

Antigone sings you deserve a break today

two cars collide head-on outside on St. James St.

a child emerges hysterical as frenzied gulls
circle the stone tables

a Pepsi can replaces the Campbell's Tomato soup

we had a room next to Mirror Lake but
it rained the morning we wanted to canoe

Montale still returns as if from Lake Como
or an Italian seacoast where it appears
he can smell lemons, or see their blossoms

and nearly understand the world.

I take this to mean leaving for good or worse
you're all dressed up and leaving your purse
on the lake shore as a tie to the world that
stops at the water's edge.

At any rate you walk in as we laugh to ourselves at your
audacity.

You begin to disappear.
Your floral dress balloons around your head
as if in a movie made for television.

Watching your descent, speechless, wiping
crumbs from our mouths in turbulent sunlight.

It is abundantly clear this is a literary day.

One on which revelations occurred to members
of all sorts of canons. Booming light.

How could anything be wrong with this massive spring?
No. Nothing is wrong. This munificent day *will* not turn
to ruins by her exploit. She *must* be swimming behind
those rocks Yes, she *is*, a crazy Jane
full of *carpe diem*.

Chagall

A single night dreams
of swollen blue stars big as goats
roosters, they float like colloids
in air, boneless

clouds grow over with laughter
of soldiers, an officer shoves
an old man into a pigsty

his silver complexion the colour
of herring, now covered in mud
and feces.....

he uses shavings of chalk
to lighten colours and olive oil
to thin paints

giving flowers body
as bodies flower airborne
malleable as angels

floating, float

just thinking of them.

Ending the Contract that Begins with I, 1964

I being in the sound of noises next door of people
making love, take to heart this erasable bond
to bathe in the empty wake of years the blank
passion I left unrecognized figuring it would
not add up to much
week-ends emptied writing epitaphs in retreat
as if the present were mine while all the indications
point to life elsewhere
the present is black, it does not move
the present is dark and

I leave it to its absence
to its pointless distribution of thoughts
about family life, and the few furtive
sexual stirs for others

I leave them to themselves and
to those others who phoned and
found the line dead, to those beautiful women
with blonde, blonde voices
wanting me to perpetuate their families

I leave them with lies, recorded poems
that praise their need to be beautiful
to analysts whose relationships are never clear
I leave unsayable truths in unspeakable situations
I leave the insurance of my absence, its premium
where words can make nothing out
of especially nothing

I leave nothing more for you
whom I could never figure out
and never tried, but it is yours
to do with as you want

Franconia

We scrape admission money together.

'Imagine if you will, the apple orchard
a snow of petals. Mister Frost sits in this room
at eleven in the morning. He wears a green plastic
visor, arm bands to prevent his white shirt sleeves &
cuffs from slipping below his wrists as he composes poems.'

She leads us through other rooms that summon
pictures back from his life. Then we break away
and follow arrows, speed-reading weathered plaques.

Back at the motel, James Last emanates from the lobby
speakers. A poster on an easel announces the *SoulMates*
at eight tonite in the Maple Lounge: *Dance the Way You Did Back Then!*

For a quarter you can take a breathalyser test outside
of the bar. The bartender says it was put in after Bodica
the owner's Great Dane was called across the road and hit
by a late model Pontiac.

He says she flew like a boneless Chagall figure
floated across the sky and landed in an open field
we found her and pressed her wound with a towel
she was days dying.

Music from the Lounge was playing over the pines.

We entered our numbered room, everything pristine.
We moved to the music and danced through the room
breaking hermetic seals and tearing sanitary bands away
helping ourselves to a darkening green view from the window.

You mention the wooden indian hidden away at the back
of the unused cafeteria. *Yes, listen, he shifts through trees*
footsteps over the duff, can you hear him?

A synthesizer plays loudly, a rock beat that travels
over the woods, distant as this world.

Riding the Rivets in Eden

A crepuscular sun appears orange and evokes
a privacy that you fear sharing because

catching porn on the web (because the most advanced
techniques in graphics are revealed) and it is unremarkable
jissom that is repeated across faces frozen

empearlings

toweled away but not before a creator's vengeance
banned their tongues entwined and chased by pterodactyls

as daydreams turned ugly, like a rodeo
tossing their flickering hearts, a brahma's horns

disemboweling their ecumenical hopes
and dying into the world.

You must tell people how to live..

Frank Lloyd Wright to Anthony Quinn (c 1940)

A prizewinner, an architect that won a visit from Mexico and
Natural crantara doors open, Frank offers Anthony some coffee
Senses are honed with decorum and mastery of a long fingered pride
That designed sandy wind and cactus with Chicago elbow grease
Anthony, a little sheepish yet respectful, the scent is wood covering the steam from cups of black ground coffee. Why do you want to be an architect, Frank says, of all things far and wide, why an architect?

Anthony, imprisoned by unknowing, mumbles into his pressed white collar. What, what did you say? Mumbles into further oblivion. Mr. Quinn,

You cannot be an architect! How can you if you mumble? As an Architect you must tell people how to live, and do so in a firm authoritative voice. Out of his tweed pocket he pulls a white card, embossed, and hands

It to Anthony.

Here, take this business card, he is a voice teacher, an actor, he will teach you how to project your voice across skies and landscapes. Frank wishes him luck and sees him to the wooden doors.

Water

Days pass into infinity.
Unremarkable. In this unwarranted
Water wheel, there is nothing to speak of, really.

But, some man-made wing carries up. It's
Easy to tell, there is broken wood
And feathers of a sort that hang wet
And limp as it turns, cradled over and over.

Where is it from? And where is its body?
And stare to understand its source, its one-time
Movement from a man? Angling for balance
Between shore and sea. At any rate, it turns
Soon, it will loosen and disappear, track further
Away as days pass from one protean light to
Another.

Ballet Dancers' Feet

Are a mess of flatness
Bandages, veins purple wistaria
Dry absorbency powder, white or
Black or yellow distortions, hearts
Of a sort worn with soles that propound
To propel larger than life toward sky
A bookless exuberance

Arabesques, pas de deux, neat feet
Knitting air, unbound from gravity
That once winging it like propellers seek
To stabilize and fly – softly loom the air
But land, feet first
And stamps the metered floor
Those dogs poeticize

Their concrete life, ugly as sin that
Makes life concrete and our ugliness, beauty
To push grace through choreographic paces
Until a perfection is near and alights
Through skeleton, muscle, heart, brain
Our unravaged souls, unhidden in their feet
That love's articulate movement gives

Nanotechnology
after Bill Joy

Acts of god become explicit science
Like the limbic system, home to love
And hate; amygdala; recticular formation
Hippocampus; nexus-lexus of lifeblood
Channels through to the marrow and awakes
Our days with circuitry, rolling green hills
Of molecular compounds compounded
Engineered for seeing fresher and fresher
With new eyes
Teeth, hair, organs, artificial intelligence
Procreates

Allah, Buddha, Yaweh and their retinues
Of angels sitting in a huge clearing with
Webs prismatic light dancing, staggering
Perfumes and music, still consider this
Transition to be natural.

Mr. Martin, Pianist from Estonia, In town for a Competition, Goes for a Smoke in the Ericssons' Backyard in Calgary, Canada, November, 2000.

A bedroom, a bathroom and a piano.
        A scent of Nordic measures, clean
Pine and curiously, cinnamon that drift
        In and out of rooms, except morning
Eggs and bacon, then music sheets propped
        On the grand in their stark living room
They sit ageless and safe
        Each morning when like a monk he rises and
Resurrects them from graves with key prayers
        Companions we recall immortality, as playing
Outdistances Eros and Thanatos

Non-smokers, the Ericssons. A pail of sand with a cover
        Serves as an ashtray on the cold backporch, the backyard
Is dusted with a late November snow and he begins pacing and smoking, eyes
        A hibernating garden, sprigs like latent notes and there
A cold clear smell, hears a spying noise that pads behind a tree beyond the garden
        An opalescent eye stares directly at him, perhaps as direct, raw and
As beautiful as composers when they first heard the music
        Before the notes were ever written down.

December 20th 2000 And A River

Our feature presentation edges from first springs, some
Recognition of words mouthed and thirst sets in, a mortal
Taste that initiates to picture to dream its beginnings through
Thickets least resistance and flow in gathering both throng
And splice of earth and galaxy, of garnet and bloom to horizons
Not clock-aware hands that circle every day and night, but born
In mind's heart and mind that graced a first mote that begins
A first rain and then to drink from that time's meteoric stream
That grows and gathers momentum and speed in extraordinary ways
As imagination makes memory and vice-versa, rolls through a lifetime
Blood's extensive synapses toward furrow, convolution and aorta that
Makes light worth living in.

day after day, cormorant-looking referees
in suits dive into an ordinary grey ocean
of buildings to enhance or delay homeostasis
it averages out however and depends
on determination to enact desire and suffer
accordingly
but on the surface it is wonderful
mechanisms and machinations
that strive to increase an understanding
overcome setbacks (some give in to
where pain obliviates an inability
to fly, or sense the repeated blare
of an oncoming train) and
ponder beauty, its time and space
that occupies purpose
a tendency to suggest more than
its evanescent curves that embody
some perpetual motion mind needs
to master beyond training-wheel thoughts
shaky points of origin
in caves, astral calendars
unraveled, to keep appearances alive
with progress, and so on and on we go.

Matt Santateresa
is the author of *Combustible Light*.
He lives and writes in Montreal.